Considerate lessons for life

BAVI AHDEN

BLUEROSE PUBLISHERS
India | U.K.

For permissions requests or inquiries regarding this publication, please contact:

BLUEROSE PUBLISHERS
www.BlueRoseONE.com
info@bluerosepublishers.com
+91 8882 898 898
+4407342408967

ISBN: 978-93-5819-161-5

Cover design: Muskan Sachdeva
Typesetting: Pooja Sharma

First Edition: August 2023

Dedication

"If you believe in success and handwork it's remarkable to be a better person first and not to be a villain and win."

I dedicate this book in remembrance of my mother and father who left me in such a young age.

"There is a quote after them I was taught that"

The Lord is everything.

The Lord cares.

The Lord loves.

The Lord makes

everything beautiful

so

"LOVE LORD"

Foreword

I am giving these words to touch others' lives. Being authentic and always open to receiving and also giving. That's not just some words but can change others' way of thinking towards their day-to-day life. It's a good description of lessons that not only senior people but also can change younger children's life. One who feels low to one who wants to enhance their knowledge.

And while they may live and work in different fields, they all share the same knowledge to live life in a better way.

This book captures the eyes of people who want to approach to a healthy living. This is written as a Leader in which, I gave my experiences known as the "new thought".

The major purpose of this book is to increase knowledge among people so that they can find themselves, whether in their careers or in their personal lives, to use their common sense and generate new ideas for their lives and live a great and healthy existence.

Preface

A few lines in the explanation of the object and origin of this book may not be out of place by the preface to its contents.

In 2019, these thoughts and experiences came into my life which I wanted to share with people out over the globe.

I thought it right to collect the topics of all my life span and had this permanent record on this important subject of life and about the life lessons for the humans who want to create their life in the best way and understand their own behaviours that to do good and be good no matter what, and the way life goes on. I was and I am always getting inspired by my Guru.

Those words can be used as a guide to the ones who want to get positive moods and lessons in life.

Hopefully, this paper can help the readers to expand their knowledge about living a better life and get lessons for doing good and facing the challenges of life remain to go forward even in a negative situation.

"To you it's grace,
you have in your trace.
Be in a good company,
to make this symphony.
Value it takes,
if you merge in your space".

“Fame is useless,
knowing yourself is priceless.

Saw the leaves waving with the wind you blow,
felt to catch the embrace to make it show.
The beauty I feel is so pure,
you know better what it takes for sure.
High up high down,
the words of crown.
Do good,
Be good.
That's what we should know.

In this modern world everyone wants something,
and to ascend above all,
we can accomplish greatest,
heights by our docile demeanour.

Contents

Motivation about Time

In life time, is very important. How you spend it, it is a difficult task in a whole day; you always need to have a positive mindset to spend it wisely. According to many experienced people I met with they always suggested me that being on time and doing everything on time play a very vital role in our lives basically we need to always focus our day according to time. when we do all our work on time it gives fruitful seeds to our life, believe me if you start your day early and leave your bed early, you will experience a different life altogether and also if you are with the right people by your side than its all awe- inspiring and very rare we find them, the friends, the people we work with and the family because they all have their different mindsets and different thinking experiences of life. I know it's difficult to wake up early, but if you guys do and make yourself particular at and take a decision, you won't believe you will have more time to focus on new things and planning your life schedule, never depend on others but depending on yourself is fruitful, always believe in yourself because believing in yourself is something that you are giving power to yourself and then all goes well. Firstly, think who you are, why you are on this planet because that is the most valuable question you will ask from the universe and then time goes right.

It's your time to take yourself to the next level. If you can't fly run, if you can't run walk. If you can't walk crawl, but whatever you do you have to keep moving. Remember that. Help yourself and make your time valuable. It's time to show how bad you want your dreams to be fulfilled. From to-do list to shaping your destiny. It covers everything. You need to change your habits. Remind your child always that how important the time is, doing everything on time is so important. Whether you are studying in a school, work, appointments or any activities. We have to remind us this motivation about time to our self. When it comes to getting results, it takes motivation. Motivation makes things happen and wonder can happen. We need to understand this that how this time is precious in whole day. As you think how you can utilize your time, you will be able to master your life.

Some famous quotes on time motivation.

1."*We live in deeds, not years in thoughts, not breaths, in feelings*

Not in figures on a dial. We should count time by heart throbs. He

Lives who thinks most, feels the noblest, acts the best." **- Aristotle**

2. *'Learn to enjoy every minute of your life.*

Be happy now. Don't wait for something outside

Of yourself to make happy in the future. Think

How really precious is the time you have to spend?

Whether it is at the work or with your family.

Every moment should be enjoyed and savored.

- Earl Nightingale

So, as also said by some famous people above it is very important to be on time, because time is limited so why not make it valuable. Have the courage to follow your heart and intuition and move forward to change your life for a better future, and it is always in your own hands.

Are We Thanking Enough?

BE thankful for everything you have in your life because whatever you have received from the God is already a Gift that you deserved and your thought process bought you, many times we feel frustrated that we don't have this and that, but Believe me if you guys have a positive way of living and be thankful for everything you have, you will have more energy to have more positive and valuable things in life.

So, in my opinion and experience we should always be thankful. We always think sometimes that everything is going wrong, but we should always see well in everything may be its somehow building you for better days in your life. Take a look, sit for a while and think about yourself and see the better side in everything and then take a decision that what you have to do? Are you thankful enough? All are blessings if see from a positive mind and always shut when anything negatives comes just make it positive at the right time when you hit by negative, feels great and be thankful.

Let's lighten up every cell in our body and be thankful. Imagine yourself filled with this beauty. Illuminating energy and seeing everything as positive Believe that there is beauty in everything we have. Believe in the passive step of creation, which is all around us. Happiness is a state of being that comes from within. Always be thankful. This life is meaningful if we see it through the lens of positive energy. Use your eyes to see! Use your ears to listen! Use all your senses and be thankful that you have eyes to see, ears to listen, and all these senses. Be thankful. Say thank you to the universe, which brings you everything when you need it. Thanks lord. Everything we have, we should be thankful for because it was given to us when we gave all our positive energy to get it.

The truth will set us free. All the suffering and pain will vanish if we are thankful enough! Why desire more materialistic things? It will not go with you when you depart. Be thankful every time. A big change will occur in your life. Sometimes the new path will not be so easy, but try and go ahead, and you will be thankful. If you are thinking that you have nothing, then you should see that you have your hands, with which you can work, and your legs, with which you can walk.

We should be thankful for all these things which we have already instead of sitting and looking at your phone and things I don't have this and I don't have that as looking at other people lives. Remember that! You have everything be happy and be thankful. Some people don't have anything, see them they are still enjoying. So why not you can enjoy by what you already have. See yourself and think about it and grow.

Reality

Let us see the Reality. What we see in our television screens is not always the reality because that already captured by the particular people who have acted at a particular day, but we try to see it again and again and think that this is the reality although reality is something different because the life we are in and living that is the actual reality based on false screen plays we forget what is actual going in our lives and ourselves, whatever we see we become like that very rare people know this and very rare people understand this.

And gradually we grow with life we start to understand this. We should always see and observe things which are going around means in improving yourself. Well I am not talking about looking at other people lives. I will laugh here because that is laughable.

Try to figure out where you can improve whether in relationships or your work or with the people you talk much, if someone is not talking to, don't force them to talk although try to understand what the fault you are making that the other person is behaving like that means check yourself first and to judge other this is the reality. looking at your television screens sometimes the person next to you, you forget to have a word with them or to listen to them and also while watching we behave different or rude to the other person to not to disturb. Always listen, listening can change your life and behave according to that and improve yourself and others next to you.

What to see you become, if you see bad things you will attract bad things, if you are looking for good things. Good will comes to you and you will become good. We can see good inspirational things in television. Which will inspire you to do something like that, maybe it will improve you as well and you will learn something new. To receive something good you need to focus on good too. Television brings lots of things, kind of we are putting garbage in ourselves for bad things which we see, like if we see anger and we will become like that, so avoid those kinds of visions. It will distract your state of frequency and might trouble you in life. Avoid such things. Talk to people around you, get to know each other's and learn something new. Be happy in your family and enjoy with them. So, see the realities of life and become a better person.

Tiny Thoughts

Tiny thoughts which we think always. In my opinion tiny thoughts are always makes us sad right? Always think beautiful and big because if you think beautiful things like of flowers, kids, nature, you will feel better and calm. Instead of looking in TV or mobile why not, look at nature, which is so beautiful and amazing.

Just side everything else, try to love nature and keep a calm and beautiful mind. Just open a calm sound by your side and have a look to plants, water them whether you are in a park or at your roof top, look at the sky raise your arms, feel the air, fresh air, listen to the sounds of the birds, birds sounds makes you feel better and sweetness will be pouring in. We all have a child inside, so feel free and enjoy that moment for even one hour of your day. Look at the beauty, which is always with you but you are ignoring it and instead looking at the people only and your phones. Make your life different and make a difference in your life. Happiness depends on us. You Change the path of your life every single time if you think good it will bring you light. Fill your life with the positive.

Gratitude, love, kind thoughts, words, and actions bring light to our lives. Focus on it. If you have a friend you can talk to him or her, for you desire and thinking to do or to share your things. To create your tomorrow, go to your bed tonight and think good moments of your life which you have spent. This will make you happy and make you at peace. Be blissful. It's all in you and you can change your tiny thoughts to the positive and enjoy a great life ahead.

Tune your frequency of the universe of pure thoughts. There should not be hate in you, bring love inside you and love everyone. This is good to know your inner being and focus on more valuable things which can bring you happiness. Remember that life is always moving. Move ahead. The aim of life is self-development. To realize yourself completely. This is true gift you will give to yourself. Try to compliment others. life will mirror back to you what you will give to others.

Appreciate people, laugh more, and bless your money.

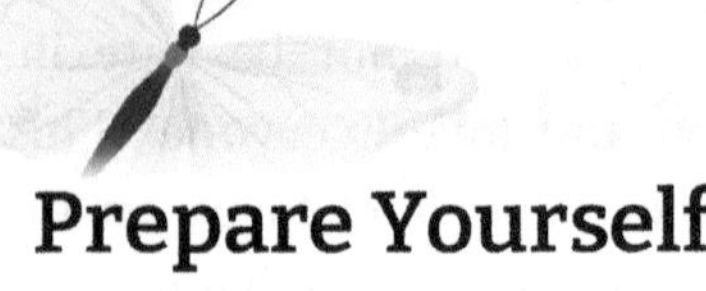

Prepare Yourself

Prepare ourselves before doing anything important?

We always need to prepare ourselves because preparation is something, which gives an accurate outcome to something, which we will do or think. It is important to prepare whether you are at work or preparing for exams or you are preparing something new to eat or explore.

Many times, we do not prepare ourselves, which makes us and let us to get to fail. Here the suggestion is preparing something before doing anything will lead you to success, which is, also important to life whether we are in any business, homework or schooling includes studies or anything!

Make sure you do prepare, here is an example like if you going to give a speech on stage you need to prepare yourself for it because if you don't prepare maybe you lack some points which you wanted to express but you could not because you were not prepared. Make notes or write down in a dairy, which is also a preparation, which will lead you to be perfect. We always think why the other person is so successful. This is the great question. Why? The answer is found in the unhappy disposition of the individual. Moods have something bad things tens of thousands. Clean up your moods!

This is the best slogan of the successful person. Every condition is worthwhile. We can set ourselves for the things which can lead us to the success in life. Prepare for it. Prepare yourself. Gentleness, patience, consideration for others brings you good opportunities for life. They build up a personality that has one hundred percent of attracting force in you. We can be small, narrow, and faultfinding with our hands against all others. Respect others and Respect yourself these are the words of a successful person. People will tolerate us but they will not desire us. Be prepared for everything in life. We can set up to clean up this endless little weakness of our dispositions and improve ourselves. Be prepared for your life and be prepared for everything.

Anger

Anger!! It always feels peculiar when see this word? Right. We all feel somehow in our lives, but what should we do to overcome it, always count on 10 before speaking in anger because it will tell your mind something good that see your mistakes or see from others mindset or think that it will hurt your body so we should always control it.

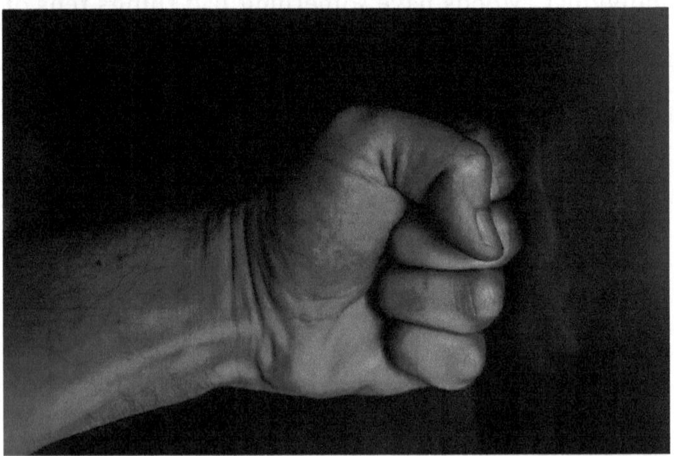

Sometimes kids gets angry, listen to your kids, you know we should always have to see things most sweetly, if other person is angry it means it's his or her problem, you should not get effected by it because this is their problem and we can only do one thing that to solve it by discussing the matter not to get angry at the same time with the same frequency the other person has? Right? Be sweet at that time and see the changes how it will slow down the other person or maybe he or she will realize his mistake or her mistake.

So, what you have to get by these words that always try to calm yourself when the other person is angry. I tell you one incident happened with me, one day I was standing on the roadside, I saw many people got caught up in traffic, everybody wanted to go first and no one had the patience in them. I was standing very calm and I was happy and a sweet smile was there on my face and suddenly one lady was shouting from her window sitting in the car that move! Move! and she was angry because she doesn't have enough patience to wait. So suddenly she got to a chance to see at my face and I was very calm and her anger got controlled. So, you know what always be calm when someone is angry may be your vibrations will also calm them with sweetness.

Have a Shine Inside

The Shine inside us, there is always a shine inside us, which makes us shine so bright if we follow the good habits, take good teachings in life and always be true and positive. You should have empathy for others and you should adequate others to smile anyhow.

Be respectful, polite or considerate in manner. Which will lead you to grow and makes other happy? You feel like wriggled. Do endeavor, forbid bad habits, and become shiny bright. Become dexterous and illustrious and everlasting and endless happiness which will follow your way no matter what, it's not easy though but putting your effort can change anything. There are many classes and books you can find ways to meditate. Another way is to sit quietly and observe the breath. Make a song out of your affirmations and sing them with joy. You should reduce to have negative thoughts. Do whatever you can to make your transformational change a joy and a pleasure. Have fun! Love others and love yourself. Blaming only gives away our power. Be ready for love when it does come. Prepare the field and be ready to nourish it.

Never make your mind desolate make it hysterical for yourself, don't misjudge anyone always keep a positive mood and positive energy within you. Be jovial Meet new people and eradicate all your negative thoughts and energies. Be idolized. Inside each and every person are all the good qualities.

Your Consciousness will either keep you there or lift you to a better position. It is all up to you. Be good and do well.

Speak Less and Listen More

Something, which is very important in life, that is, speak less and listen more.

Just close your eyes for a minute and think, how much you have spoken today and where you did not listen, when your mom spoke or friends or your dad or anybody in the house and how you reacted there? Did you really listen or passed the comment on it? It is always that someone is telling us something important only if it is right not bad habits I am telling here, that what you have to analyze because there are good things in the world and bad things too. It's your decision to judge that if it is good and better for you then I think, you should listen first react according to your judgment. There are two things you have to remember listening first will always benefit you and that requires patience within you.

Whether we are talking with someone on phone call or messages or talking to a person sitting next to you. In addition, immediately you learn something new, it always said try something for 21days and you will master of it. Therefore, it is better to speak less and listen more. When the other person finishes then try to express your words. Think of a rose from the time it is a tiny bud. Love roses? They are beautiful when you hold them. Feeling of love. Awareness and knowledge, we gain we do things differently. And now it is the time to learn new in your life and get knowledge. Listening is a powerful virtue you can have if you do so. We are living in the world, where all wants to speak and speak and nobody wants to listen. We are responsible for ourselves. We are frightened, insecure, or scared. Understanding will bring you compassion. The only things we could possibly teach ourselves which we have already been taught. Stop for a moment and catch your thought. You are a power being in your world. Each moment is a new beginning. This moment is a point of power! This is the moment where change begins! Yes! You darling try to listen and react. You are the only person who can make that change in you. Do that.

Always Refrain From Lying

Always refrain from telling a lie. More to the fact, if it is to save others do lie sometimes for better, which should not hurt anybody.

Very difficult task living in this kind of generations, but it can be possible if possibly done. Worth is always in it. Have always a zeal in yourself to do something better for yourself. What we get by telling a lie, what if the other person gets to know that you lied to them and they caught you. The impression will be embarrassing. Right or wrong? So always speak true. Many a times we never see things clearly that telling a lie can ruin your relationship with the other person who trusted you. Being a part of society, we should think that telling a lie can harm our own reputation. Which leads to make us sad? Be true to yourself and be true to others.

Always hinder yourself from telling a lie. Lean against truth that is obvious being true will always kudos! It will be extremely good. That will also be a considerate act. Always be candid in nature. Yes of course be obedient too. Be a person that you want to become. Genuinely give your life a true meaning. Change for the life which you have and make more beautiful by being a true person.

Hardships come in life but if you be true it will be easy to overcome and also you will see tremendous change in yourself. Try to be chaste and generous.

Telling lies can also trouble you sometimes so it is always said, be true.

Alcohol

Alcohol addiction. I know many people intake, even the new generations started to intake ignoring the fact that it can ruin their body, mind and soul.

It is always said that if a person drinks, his or her mind start to numb for that particular time and they never able to focus for the right, whether he or she taking small amount of it or large, they are taking it to slow down their stress or they just want to forget the world around for a while, but what happens- disaster for their lives and the lives of those who are around them.

This body is divine. If we wash it with GOD praises it can also be cured or give you a better life and solve your problems too, which will make you strong as well. However, the generations do not understand this because of their company they keep and with them; they are already ruining their lives. Company matters a lot! Because if you are with a person who drinks, you will somehow start to drink as well for pleasure, which is completely wrong because we should always have to see that in which company we are in. Is it good for us or not or maybe it will affect our future?

Running to the fact that it can ruin your family atmosphere, your life, your kids. Kids are also learning from their parents? Not they?

I have seen many girls have also started drinking, when they just lost their mind. One incident I tell, where I saw a girl just came out from an auto rickshaw she was completely drunk, I was standing there looking for an auto rickshaw wherein I found somehow this Auto standing and I asked this auto driver if he wants to take me to the destination. It was a day time, auto driver said that he cannot go because the girl who is standing there is asking me to take her to her home but she doesn't even know where her house is, because she was fully not in the condition because she drank excessive drink. Auto driver was also very confused what he should do? Just say I am healthy and whole and complete. Assume that you are already in the process of healing. Heal yourself to not have alcohol again. Which is not good for your health? Make a room for the new beginning in life. Realize and accept that I was the only person responsible for my own health. Be in bliss. We must take care of our family. And do good deeds. Be in a good company. You should not give punishment to yourself and others. Which can ruin your life and your family? Always think that before taking it that it is harmful for you and your body. Rejoice with others.

So, see how it is affecting the generations, we should not focus on wrong things, when we are in trouble. We should see for other positive things, which can improve us or overcome our situations. It is not with women only it is with growing kids and men as well, Men are more into it. Keep quitting it and have a happy life for yourself and the people around you. It is a danger to life. Get out of that danger and have a better place inside you.

Discipline!!! Are We All Disciplined??

Discipline is the key to our success and this is always true, whether you deny it or not. It is important for all the people and age groups. Self-discipline is something students should have and, in our lives, because it is truly important and it is not a commodity one can buy from the market.

Whether you are in your house or working outside or in any part you are playing in your life. It should always be disciplined. Its makes you excellent in everything you do with concentration which will turn you to achieve an aim in life.

Nothing can prevent us from attaining our goals in life. Yes of course without the support of God you won't be able to achieve anything. With self-esteem and discipline, you can also achieve academic excellence. All what is needed, is practice because practice makes a man perfect, it is always said. You must think that you are open to a wonderful new position. One that uses all the talents and abilities. I LOVE WHAT I'M DOING. We are all capable of being a perfect person. I think it is our bright and natural way to think that we can get success to all our life. It is said, "If a first you don't succeed, try, trying, try again. Divine intelligence gives us all the idea when we need. It's doesn't matter how long we are thinking of ourselves as a failure. There is lot more than success is hiding between those words which we use like I AM A FAILURE. But change that because YOU CAN BE A WINNER. These seeds will grow into an abundant harvest. The principles are the same.

Discipline is something which can take you to see things in a better way. Yes, it is difficult but is there, is there anything, which can be attained easily? If we discipline ourselves for some particular things like now days, we look to our phones so many times. Right? We can make a plan and make ourselves busy in other things so that we can be disciplined to not see our phones uselessly for many times in a day and instead we should look around.

Be Slow and Steady

How we can win by being slow and steady. Success comes to those who are slow and steady in their work. It is not always necessary to complete any work fast in order to win. Whether you are driving a Vehicle or anything. If you are in a hurry to reach your destination any wrong turn can cause an accident.

Just the same when we start to learn any sport or new work. If you hurry, you won't be able to learn it that good which you can learn slowly. Just like the hare in the race with the tortoise. Even clever people who work speedily may fail if the work is done in fast. Just take an example, a student who just studies only just before an examination. He is never regular in his true studies, that he will not going to score that much or he may get fail in exam.

Nothing is gained by being hasty and careless. It is better to be slower and more careful in one's work. Those who think hastily sometimes make many mistakes. So always be slow in whatever you are going to accomplish. It is always better to be slow and steady. We cannot gain anything in being fast, slowly everything gains and we tend to win.

Work your things in patience. Then you can succeed in life and every part of your life.

There Is Always A Way for Everything

There is always a way for everything in life. We always think that there is no way but if we see from very positive mind then there is always a way. Take that line for granted and understand the way of life.

Always be positive and see things from deepest analysis. It is always said that meditate for better outcome. Meditation can also heal you and make you calm; it takes away the stress in you. Thousands of years ago, people used to meditate a lot and even now, a day's people have understood that meditation is something, which will sooth you. So, whenever you feel sad, you need to meditate, see there is always a way for everything. You can read good books, which will enhance you in a better way and it is always said that books are our best friends rather than anything else.

You can also choose someone whom you can trust and who is trustworthy to you.

Don't be dumb, always smile and wash away your useless worries. There are always better days. Everything passes away which troubles you and will be your past in the future. So always think that there is always a better way to everything. Rejoice in the abundance of being able to awaken each morning and experience a new day. Be glad to be alive, to be healthy, to have friends, to be creative, to be living in harmony. Enjoy your Transformational process. Begin to realize Prosperity everywhere and rejoice in it. If you see well-dressed people, think, isn't it wonderful that they have so much abundance? There is plenty for all of us. Be creative. Rejoice in the small things and new Beginnings.

So always look for a vision which will enhance your boredom to success.

Changing Moods

What mood is? Hey any clues, well moods, it changes in minutes, don't they?

Happy mood, sad mood, angry mood, dumb mood, smiley mood, nerd mood and many moods a person faces, actually we all faces...

Which mood you like the most? All will go to say it is obviously happy and smiley mood.

How to get smiley or happy mood, hey you! It is all inside you. We never searched ourselves. Are we searching ourselves? No. There is always a gem inside you, if you explore it by searching in you. Often, we look inside others, but what we get? We sometimes hurt ourselves. Instead, look for yourself. This is not good, bad this is not right, or wrong it is just we know inside as home. We also tend to recreate in our personal relationships the relationships with our mother and fathers. We also treat ourselves the way our parents treated us. We scold and punish ourselves in the same way. So, change can heal your life. It is the way what we think about ourselves and about our world. Do not frustrate your life. Release it.

Looking in yourself may tell you a lot of things and might you get changed in the process and everything is wonderful but by our own moods makes it different, don't worry about things, today it is difficult, tomorrow it will be easy. Enjoy life and have fun. Say all is wonderful, all is wonderful and see the magic in few days, all will be wonderful in your life and you will see how happy you are in every sphere of life. Take it easy and go with the flow and encourage others and yourself that this situation will go away. It's you just keep your moods scrubbing away and soon you have a pan as good as new. Cleaning the mental house after a lifetime indulging in negative mental thoughts is kind of eating all the time junk food and not getting any benefit. Always you to keep in mind that willing to change are a great process of changing. Just keep doing the new affirmations and soon you will have totally cleared old limitations in you. These bodies and mind can be healed. Let us always do something to dissolve it. Go to the mirror and look deep into your eyes, touch face and cheeks. In addition, say to yourself "I am going to release my negative thoughts and enjoy my day. Whenever we look into the mirror today, most of us will say something negative to ourselves. We either criticize our looks or berate ourselves for something. Never ever do that. Always make a positive declaration about yourself it is the quick way to make yourself happy.

Never Give Up

Never ever give up for what you are doing. It is always said that giving up is something dumb which you will gonna do, please never give up. Whether you are putting in your work, exercise to lose weight or making a perfect body, never give up. If you have just started, don't worry go slowly but never give up. Never stop trying, never stop believing in yourself, never give up and then your day will come and everything will seem so amazing to you, so never give up even for one minute.

Never give up because great things take time and whether you are ill don't worry one day will come and you will be fine. Not every day is the same there are plenty of things in the world and work for your dream.

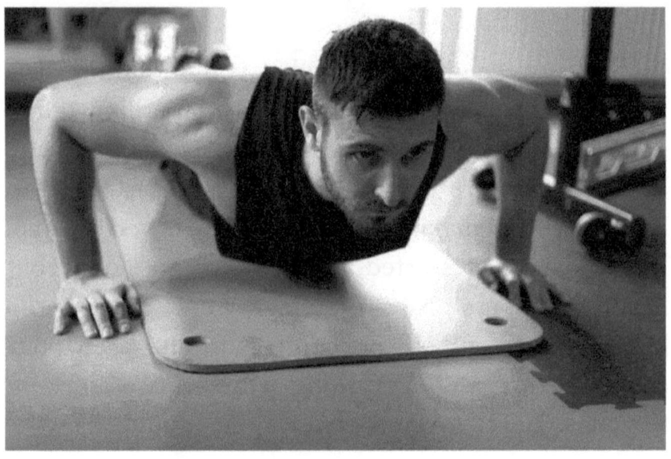

Your hardest times often lead you to the greatest times of your life. Just keep going where you are going because that will lead you to your destiny and you will be happy to see the success, don't give up, just go on, on and on.

Do not fear anything but rather face it when the going get you tough just look for the sky and move forward, God will help you and he helps everyone even if we not even remember God, he still helps, God is merciful. Gather courage to believe that you can succeed. It does not matter how many times you will get fail, never give up! Stand up and face it. On the same journey, if we look deeply into every life that touches our own. It is plain that everybody is filled with one great purpose, which stands for all. Peace, power and plenty at every point in our human existence. There is no tomorrow, so do it today and prove yourself to the best of everything.

The one who fails and gets up again is a hero in my sight. Always have a hope. Stay strong, stay positive and move with all your potential.

Never give up! Do not let your mental state tell you to stop but move forward with your steps, which you have taken for the journey to be succeeded. And there is always a will. We can change anything by changing our state of mind. So never ever, give up!

WORK
FOR
IT

Sports

About sports. If you ask me, which sports I prefer you to play is football game tremendously amazing, it feels good when we play any sports. Football is a complete game. You can play any sport badminton, volleyball, handball and many more. However, football is something which will make you strong enough to live a life wherein you face many hardships. Sports should be there in life of everyone whether that person is old or a child. Sports make a person strong and disciplined in every sphere of life.

You feel more active and enjoy being with your teammates and learn from them as well. Never be so over confident because we should always KEEP a decent key in our behavior, because it leads you to grow more.

Everyday challenges and training make you strong and awe-inspiring. We all know that sports is something which makes you smile and happy all the time, sometimes you do not even want to come back home from playing sports even if your parents say let's go home. That is laughable. A hobby gives us pleasure for we do it for the love of the work and not under the pressure to earn. Enjoy all games and sports. All we need to have passion for what we are doing. We can give full potential to it. You may also give the idea of bringing glory to the country you are playing for. Victory is possible if we enjoy our sport and also encourage our team mates.

If you play professionally than, it is truly awesome, playing with other teammates is difficult and encouraging like you are in a war.

Also, challenges you to win but we should not always think of winning because there are times where you will lose as well, but that doesn't mean you should quit, instead go on with the flow and make yourself more into it. Do handwork and see the results.

I personally play football sport. I feel so much good when I am in the ground. Greenery everywhere and the sky full in bloom, when you see that you feel special and grace with all your teammates and coaches. I think you should go for sports, once you enroll, you will see how it is important, it make you stress free and for once you forget the world, enjoy, and win. So I think it is beneficial for us and we should opt for it.

Never Be Upset

Something, which is very important in life, that is always not to be so upset. Why? Because it is not good for you and your health and for others in your families as well.

Why to be upset, if we should know that everything is moving according to our karma. So always stay positive. And think good thoughts because there is always positive in everything. You can do one thing that you can talk to your friends or you can play with kids, no matter of what age you are, kids always make us happy.

It's always good to spend time with kids, because they are more joyous then us or you can spend time with your grandparents because they are experienced and they can teach you or tell you their experiences. Not everyone is equally alive in all ways, but it is up to us that we can change our state of mind and forget the past. The great wide, beautiful world with the wonderful waters around it, see that, feel that, sky, sun, water, moon everything is so beautiful. If you get upset that your boss is rude to you. Just be easy, it is everywhere. So, leave here, face it, be soft, and work, because you are here to work. It is possible to go through life. Concentration is the first step towards our direction. I have watched the people in the work world. I was first guest in the new little house. The true self knows and knowing do not turn aside; perhaps hold it fast and say that ' YOU CAN OVERCOME ANYTHING'

No one can ever hope for success. Be yourself! Do the thing you can do in your own way. That is your secret and your success. There is no use striving after anything. There is no use to mourn after anything. Happiness and unhappiness are the conditions of the mind and have nothing to do with real life. We know that happiness is the law of life and our natural condition. It is not our own lives that make us unhappy it is our fear of what others will think of us. True path is right for us as well as others.

Often, we only spend time with our computers or work. But spend time your kids, they will make you happy.

Worry not always, every day is a new day and a new beginning and time changes and we make new friends and get together with families.

Say hi to new people and enjoy their company. In addition, enjoy your own self as well, it is always important to love yourself first then to love others because if you are happy they will be happy too.

Keep a positive environment. And have a happy life. It feels our souls filled with the greatness of growth. All is happiness is in ourselves if we find it within us.

Work Hard

Work hard, we know that if we work hard the fruits of life will flourish and we will have plenty of peace later. Actually, work hard in the background. Enjoy what you are doing. Enjoy every moment, you never know when your life will have grace.

Reading can free your mind from all the sad and negative. Always keep a positive book with yourself. Because reading books will give you positive aspects in life. You can read books that encourage you.

Working with team, will also make you successful. Developing strong focus can also let you to work hard and with team mates it's truly amazing and you can grow more. You have the power to bring light to people's lives. You can work hard in anything. Mostly love who you are and always get excited about who you are becoming. Behave well with your teammates, encourage yourself and them.

Work hard in the background. People will see you succeed at the end. Never forget to cheer for yourself. Never forget God because with God everything is possible. Without God we are nothing.

Hard work even if you is women. Women can do anything, they have power actually they are the same as men. Hard work makes you perfect! With time, management and decision you can move brightly. Enjoy doing hard work which will give happiness later. Mark the words.

Take Proper Care

Take proper care of yourself. If you take proper care of yourself, you can be happy and healthy. Be kind to those who are not even kind to you, smile, life is all about how we take ourselves and how we take proper care of ourselves. Sometimes in life, everything goes smoothly and sometimes-unexpected things happen.

The important knows how to turn those problems into solutions. Never lose hope. Move and move and move no matter what your condition and take proper care. At the end of the day, your biggest competition is you. Have faith and hope. Indulge yourself into your self-care. And take care of those who are around you.

Whatever happens do not loose hold of the two main things in life is hope and faith. They will lead you to go further no matter what. Never stop thinking positive and take proper care of you. Appreciation must be sincere. Your voice, your eyes, your body language all reflects your true feelings. In order to get real appreciation, we must get real love into our hearts and teach how to connect with our words. Words, which brings happiness in you and others. There is a great truth in the power of thoughts. You need to be expressive. Then each life is great in itself. The life and love and God are one. There are qualities of mind and heart and person too. Benefit of mankind in general.

Do not struggle instead have a positive mind and move forward. Moving forward will excite you to face the challenges in life. Taking proper care of your mental health is very important; it's only you who can change it. So, change. Just change, do not worry. The true self knows, do the thing you can do in your own way. No matter how anyone else does things, whatever you have around you in things or everything is a blessing because they are fulfilling the true laws of their beings. So, take care of you and the others around you. Do something for your personal care. Eat good food. Do yoga or exercises to make you fit and happy.

Speak Good

Always speak well because when you speak well, everyone wants to be with you. And it shows that how much you are sweet and a person to whom other wants to be with. I have also experienced the same. You can also change yourself by speaking well always. Choose words which are good unlike other words like the abusive words now a day people use. Don't you feel uncomfortable talking and be with those kinds of people who only speak with adding abusive words. Never be with those kinds of people because words are something that shows your character. Moreover, character is very important for a person to build in the society. Choosing right words can change your entire life which will have lots of good friends around and it feels good when someone says, I like that person because he or she has the character and I like to be with those kinds of people, because you also learn something good from them.

Speaking good, keep a smile on your face can lead your character stronger and which makes you a valuable person. It is necessary that you should not judge someone because judging someone is not a good habit. No matter what we want to do, we must work it All-out in our mind exactly as we want it to be. Have a plan-think, speak and be the thing itself. We can be small mean and narrow. We can change that to better. It is in our hands. People will tolerate us, but they will not desire us, so be sweet and soft. Our own room is preferred to our own company. We lose our value in every respect. So, use your words and actions wisely.

Always one thing in life, you will meet many people in your life but very few rare are good and true.

Always check your friends circle and check if you need to be with that person or not because choosing right people for yourself is also important.

Speak good and nice makes a very big difference. Character is something, which is very difficult to, built in the society and does good things and never make fun of others uselessly. Have fun but be with good company friends. Making good friends is a plus point and enjoyable. So always speak good buddies and see the results. Never be angry for your own wrong words which you use while you get angry. Always be calm and happy.

Respect Others and Your Parents

Respect others and your parents. Yes, respect others and your parents. It is important in life. Never get irritated but see well in everything. Your elders always speak well for you, but we never listen. That is bad. They always say right for you but we sometimes deny it. God abides in your parents as well. Try to figure out what is right and what is wrong for you. Listen carefully to your parents and respect them with your heart.

Take care of yourself and them too. Never leave them to old age centers for the sake of your own benefits. Take care and respect them as in your living. Smile with them, they gave birth to you. And you are their children. They took care of you when you took birth. Why not take care of them now when they need you? Remember that always.

They taught you, took care of your studies and always wanted you to become something in life so that you should not say and repent later. Keep in mind. Taking care of others in your life is also important. ALSO, take care of your friends, which is a good sign. Make good friends and have a great life.

Very rare people have great friends, who actually help when needed. Always keep with them. Enjoy life to fullest. It is important to choose wisely your friend circle because that matters your own character as well. Take care of them, when they are not well. But we need somewhere care whether in words or anything.

Things can be better if we want to make that change. Taking care is one of the best signs of goodwill. Always think that, you are doing the good deed and which will also give you benefit later. Love yourself and others and your parents. They are precious. Like you are precious.

Following GOOD footsteps of your journey of life. Is so much respectful. Make it valuable for yourself and others.

Keep goodwill, you will have goodwill. So, respect others and your parents. In order to be happy, we must learn not to put a perverted value on life's differentiation. We have absolutely nothing to do with it. So be happy. True possession is true happiness. We can lose anything that is our own. Happiness is a magnet, attracting to it. Moreover, all the wonderful things in the world. The life that has found its own center. Be good to your parents give them happiness. Our soul is born into the higher kingdom of thought. Create good thoughts and which makes peace and happiness.

Happiness

So, what we know and we should know that happiness depends on ourselves don't you all think the same??

Happiness depends on us. Actually, we are unique, we all are unique.

You are unique and magnificent human being. You should think that always.

Sit comfortably, notice how you are feeling and relax your whole body for a while. What you think? Relax yourself. Leave your pains down for a while. Your smile is a messenger of your good will. Your smile brightens the lives of all who see it. Your smile is like the sun breaking through the clouds. Thought is supreme. Carry your beautiful face and the crown of your head high. The value of smile creates happiness. So, give others and keep yours too with you. Be a useful person. Keep your smile be splendid. To think rightly is to create. Why not create smiles in others?

For the billions of the people in the whole world you are the unique and valuable person, never feel sad instead be happy. And you will see happiness all around. Please mark the words. It is true.

Repeat the deep relaxing seven times; just say to yourself, I AM HAPPY AND UNIQUE. You will feel joy and happiness to yourself if you do that. So why not do it every hour in a day not a difficult task I am asking you to do?

Now you are more in harmony. The positive harmony. Fill your life with light of positivity! You can change your life from negative to positive, sad to happy. Yes! You can.

Planet earth needs you, that needs you that is why you are here don't you think that?? God loves you that is why you are here. TAKE GOOD ACTIONS; SPEAK GOOD WORDS, THINK GOOD THOUGHTS. Then more good things will come in your life. Your happiness is always depending on you and how you take your mind thoughts. So always, think well. Remember that.

Trying

Yes keep "TRYING"

YES, we should always keep trying no matter what goes on, how bad things go, and you are still way ahead of everyone who isn't trying.

You have the master within you and you are always being guided in every single moment in your life. Keep trying. Think of yourself and do something for yourself. When trying to get the facts, you should think that you are collecting something for yourself. Everything that is in you is our personal desires. Just ignore the all others!! We want only our true being to justify our acts. That we find it hard to get at the answers to our problems. We should stop ourselves to not to get sad for what we want. Just think first “what you are worrying about?" and "what you can do about it”? Ask yourself and resolve your life. So, banish about ninety percent of your worries by trying something for your life and work.

William games: said these words, ' when once a decision is reached and execution is the order of the day, dismiss absolutely all the responsibility and care about the outcome'

Don't stop to consider, don't began to hesitate, worry just retrace your steps. Take steps forward and try your new beginning. Encourage yourself. Never think about your problems but to move by resolving them. There comes a time when we must decide and act and never look back. That will be the true gem in you to change and try.

As William Shakespeare said “there is nothing either good or bad, but thinking makes it so" So why not we change our thinking for a while, and why not try new and amazing. You can do only if you want to try, never feel that you will fail. We should not worry about failing actually.

If you not try, you will not be able to succeed. It is always said try and try even if you fail does not matter, because trying is also an achievement. So why not try? Always think that you need to get through and these bad situations will go away. Moreover, if you endeavor, you can achieve anything in life. But first you need to try. Believe, trying something for you is a gem within. It can be anything new you can do, so just do it. Have a happy life.

Love and Kindness

Love and kindness. Yes, nice right and interesting

As well. What do you understand by the word LOVE? Wow it feels great when we talk about it and also, we feel good when it happens for anyone, not between in a girl or boy but with anything. Although we should love everything which we have that's also something special, but here I am talking about the love which we feel deep for someone or something. Like a kid love his or her parents or mom loves his baby and child.

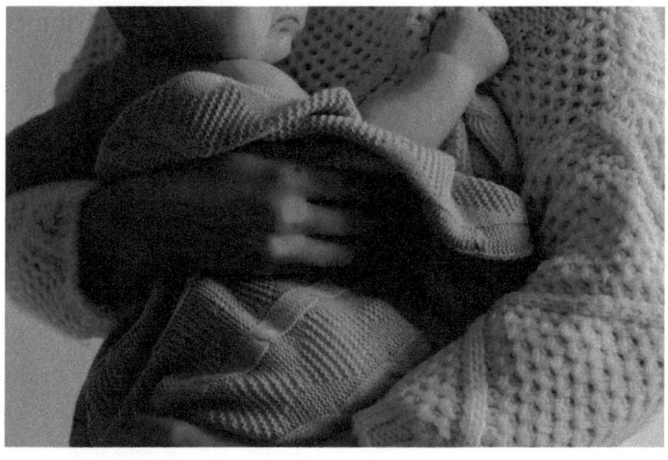

So much love she gives to the baby. Although babies are cute though. Love is a nature and can happen to anyone. You never know that you may love a dog in the house so much that when the dog is not around you even feel sad because you have so much love for the baby Dog.

Love is soft feeling. So, when we mix with kindness we love it, it becomes sweeter. Don't you think? Love is a feeling of forgiveness and makes you strong as well when you come around it. It's amazing and enjoyable. You can make more friends in two months than you can in two years by trying to get other person interested in you. People are not interested in you. They are interested in themselves. Love truly every being. Water yourself for love. Actions speak louder than words. That the expression one wears on one's faced. A baby smile can make things perfect. Become genuinely interested in other people.

The word love which you see in the picture, how you feel when you see it. That's a different vision for everyone who is looking at the picture because everyone has different love interests. Some love books, some loves their own self.

WE should love ourselves. We should. Yes, we love our materialistic things. Like cars or bikes or computer or phones etc. Love can happen in the child for his or her bicycle or love for a mate.

Love can happen anywhere. You never know between people or between friends as well. We should not take it to the one picture.

Love with your grandparents. Love with your kitty and anything which you like. Kindness makes it more beautiful because it is the feeling of love and we care for it. Make a pleasing impression on everyone you meet. Be kind. Keep this principle in mind. Thank people. Become overwhelmed and put light on others life. Give your shoulder, when they need this can change the whole mental attitude. Give your arm to hold.

So, love endlessly to whatever you love and make it kinder and sweeter so that it lasts forever and which makes you smile when you ever think about it. Enjoy every moment with love and enjoy yourself. Be kind.

Never Move in a Hurry

Never ever move in a hurry. Whether you are taking decisions or moving towards a goal. Never take any decision in a hurry, always think once before doing anything. Take a step to think for a while. Don't you think? It will be right for you. In a hurry we always skip something.

Move slowly in everything. What if we just stop for only two seconds if we are in a hurry? Relax first and move towards it. It's always good for you to analyze things better.

With time we understand the journey of life and it is good to always take a break for yourself to take any decisions about your career and all which want in your life. We are living in a society wherein everything going so fast because it's happening, no-one wants to stop for a long time, the thought process and thinking can let us take decisions better and we can move according to whatever decisions we take.

Its feel good when we think before doing our work and how it will be done. Never feel that it is not important it is crucially important for you. Managing everything and see thinks in a better way. Life is all about living and why not lives like when we are in a hurry take a little pause. That's better. Everything goes better and it will be. Stay positive and have a positive outcome.

All we know, and should know that great minds think first and move in a slow move. So, it is good to be slow and enjoy.

Creating your own decisions will make you stronger and your life will be better and you will have great outcomes. Teachable to you and others and the better days will be more powerful. Think positive and move. Great minds work slowly with patience. It is not all bad but our thinking makes it that way. Have a pause always.

Self Respect

We should all know this, and many should understand this in a life we are in. You should see yourself in the mirror and think is this person has value? Yes, you have values. You are worth. Don't you think?

Self-respect is something that is builds by us only. Keep a vision in it. Check in your life where you lack yourself worth. Always you should release people from your life who don't honor you. Yes, because you have value. You are a valuable person. Many people will purposely try to destroy you, because they may be jealous or something. Here you need to check whether these kinds of people do exist in your life. If yes just release them soon never be their slave or puppet. Remember you have worth and that is their purpose. Never be the victim of their actions. Check once, twice or even thrice if someone is doing that repeatedly which gives you stress, release that person at the very second without even thinking because you have worth. For your life is moving and it will move no matter what, if you release may be something better and more valuable on your way or if you are at home and cannot do anything? Just resolve the matter, by speaking sweet and accepting if you are wrong and the other person is right.

BE happy! Say to yourself in the mirror " I'M WORTHY" yes you are. Believe it. You are self-worth, if you are in this world. In short, respect is a positive view that you form how someone is living in their life. Cheer yourself every 15 minutes. Respecting yourself means giving yourself own worth and value, which always makes you a better person in living your life. Think about this! How it will Gonne happen? By checking your own worth. Make worthy yourself and others around you always keep that. Why not make others happy too?

Be an honest person that is self-worth. You will see changes in your life and being worth to yourself. What are the values of a person? Best actions and best to live. Do well, be good. Understandings of the good and be constructive. Check up your friends or gatherings where you feel worth, try to spend time there. Don't forget to love yourself. Loving yourself gives more power to you. Express your better way. Be calm and soft. Encouraging people is a value of a person. Do good not evil. Help others make you a valuable person and give you self-respect. So be that person which is already inside you that is waiting when you will be that. Be self-worth and have self-respect. We should not be disturbed in our old habits. The creation is too great. No matter what our desire may be, we pursue the same plan. There is always a value of smile. It happens in a flash who receives. So, smile fullest and be respected. Keep your mind on the great.

Stop Comparing Yourself to Others

Stop comparing yourself to others because if you do compare, it will not give any outcome to you if you failed to achieve what other have achieved. Comparing yourself to others always make you feel jealous because your life is something different as compare to the person who may have achieved it in putting so much hard work, it is always better to look into yourself and decide whether you can do this or not or this is meant for you or not?

I have always observed that comparing yourself to others will always lead you tired and may be in the process you stop to believe in yourself, everyone has their own qualities and experiences and handwork because in doing something new you always have to have a positive mind and tendencies to do that work with full potential it is always true every work needs Handwork. We are same humans but have different mind sets different backgrounds that's what we don't understand, once you will understand this you will start to grow. So always stop comparing yourself to others and believe in yourself.

All great lives talk, live and act according to their principles of life; understanding to each other's. This makes them one, Oneness is the highest of the high. There comes success in their lives. There are thousands of failures comes in life. Thousands of places, positions and conditions of life calls for the mature minds and the person with age and great wisdom can fill these places. Do your best never get jealous of people who have risen up powerfully to the top of their own mountains? How hard it is for any person reach the path of success. It is always not easy. Understand this. No one is to blame but we if our today narrows down to dull. The way to get something into expression for ourselves is to set about creating it for ourselves in each hour of living. We can always live peacefully by not getting jealous of anyone.

Finding ourselves in the process of life, difficult task. The personality is the workshop and our thoughts are the tools to see the divine soul in ourselves. Every individual is important. To become the visible as well the invisible power within us. We should refine ourselves. Every moment of life is important live it fully, love each other. Love yourself. The law of each life demands differently. Power, possession, attraction, name, fame, honor and success are all the desires of mind. Who have them sometimes never able to handle it? What we put into life, we take out of it. So never compare yourself to others.

Never Speak Ill of Others

Never speak ill of others. Yes, this is true and we should not speak ill of others as this makes us lower in our own self. It's when a person speaks ill of others because he or she is not satisfied with his or her own self. The person who never see things from a positive view. It is very important to speak good for others even if someone does wrong for you, it's up-to you how you take that thing inside you. It is better to speak good even for the bad.

That's a great lesson one should have in his life because that creates a new beginning to his or her life. When we speak badly for others and even think bad for others that does not make sense to your life and you are loading more negative things in your karmic account. Speak grace for others will be returned as great for you later. In life, sometimes we get what we want easily and sometimes it takes a lot of time, but that is sure that if we do and think in a positive way, then we can achieve anything. Which is grace? Changing yourself bad to the good is a difficult task altogether; however, we should look for good things. Speaking ill for somebody will make you bad and those kinds of things effects in your life. I know we all are not perfect, no one can be perfect it's only GOD who is perfect and he is merciful, if we speak polite and sweet for others without any wrong intentions inside that will be very beneficial in your life.

Create what is good and have what is right for you. Why not try once or twice and every time to improve ourselves? Speaking ill will not benefit? Will it be? The answer is 'NO'. why no, because it will not be good as you may also feel one day that you said wrong what you have said wrong to someone. Love everyone. Loving makes everything sweet and perfect. Sweet words can melt anyone. Sweetness makes grace. Be graceful and happy, you need to be happy in every situation, we all are connected whom we all meet from our past lives as per our karma, why not change your karma by not speaking and thinking bad for anyone. Love makes everything perfect. Move slowly and understand this deeply. When we sit alone and think for ourselves alone then we understand, if we keep ourselves busy every time we will not be able to understand. Remember that, so why not speak good instead of speaking ill of others. Universe knows you are ready to receive your good. Begin to be aware of it. Take time to count the stars of your life in the sky and bliss yourself for the best in you.

Enjoy Your Days Enjoy Your Life

Enjoy your days and enjoy your life. Why not smile and enjoy your life, instead of concentrating on your negative surroundings, enjoy your life, why feel sad? Hmm? Always smile no matter in which situation you are, try to smile and never take THINGS to yourself so much, everything is passing by, and this will too. One day will come if you keep calm, you will have great life. Stop blaming yourself for the things which you have not done. Make your positive. Move forward. Keep smile. And never ever argue with the person who never wants to listen to you because they will not change for anything and you will have to understand this. Enjoy your days be sweet and have a positive mind set. Does anyone feel good while being sad? No? Right? So, keep moving and enjoy your life. There are so many things in life which will keep you down but it's up to you to stand against it and be happy and make others happy by keeping calm, understand this, this will benefit you always.

There are so many things you can do by diverting your mind. Paint, whether you know or not how to paint just go ahead and paint and see after you do that you will have more interests in it or whatever hobby you have, just do that to avoid yourself from the things you can't control. Smile to others and smile to yourself in the mirror and have a happy life. Stand outside on your scooter or stand by side to your car and plug in the music, which makes you happy, I mostly prefer that we should not listen to the vulgar music instead music of nature soothing which will make more sooth. Try it that is what the master of everything, keep your calm and enjoy the music, which you have plugged in, enjoy it and smile. Does exercise that is more important or you can play with the kids outside any game with them? You will enjoy believe me. Play hide and seek with them that are so fun, will make you happy, play any sports, talk to people about good things. Start any new hobby like improve your writing or something like that.

Don't waste your life buddy. Enjoy it and let others enjoy it too. Take your decisions, because it's all in you and you can change it and have fun. Life is good if you make it good. Have a great life. Never be sad. Change that sad in you to something good, maybe it is around you and you are not looking at it.

Keep smile on your face.

Yes, it looks good on you and the people around you. Take care of you and them. It is on you how cheer you make your day when you wake up in the morning. Always keep cheering yourself in the starting of the day because the day started with a smile cheers and ends in cheers and of course you action to make it that way. All is on you. So be that change and show your day it is so valuable and you are so valuable. Keep smile. Say I LOVE TO YOURSELF much times a day. That is why I say ENJOY YOUR DAY AND ENJOYS YOUR LIFE.

Mobile These Days

Mobile these days! Yes, it is a priority now. Is it not? We all need mobile phones by our side. Yes, we all need it. Wherever we are going we need mobile gadget in our hands or wherever we want to keep it but it is always near. Why? Because we are connecting through it to the people around us and many things depends on it. Sometimes I think it's good to have a mobile phone near you and sometimes I think it is not at all good because sometimes it makes us addicted and we just chain to it. Why we just get addicted to it? Because of the entertainment around in it or we just want to distract our minds from the people around us or we just not want to see the beautiful world around us? Always this question comes around me when I see people always talking on phones and they are missing the best part. We should not capture the moment in the phone, but we should capture the moment in our minds? Don't you think? Who is reading this?

Guys it is bad and good too. I always felt that. The people who are too much into their phones are just wasting their lives. Some are attached to the other person through phone and feels that he or she cannot live without them, they actually get attached to the phone not with the person, what if that person just starts to ignore you? Will you think that your world is upside down? Some definitely will think that, but people it is not true. Wake yourself up from that dream and through these words start to grow! Your world is beautiful and never makes yourself in the cage of mobile phone. See around your own world, see that maybe you can just start a new career and that will be the proud moment for you and others like your parents. See that change in you. It will make you awesome! Great days come to those who think great and see the results. Believe it. It happens.

Moreover, it will goanna improve your health as well, use your mobile only when it is very important, not uselessly to impress another person or to see what is going on in other person's life. Hey you see your own life where you are going? Improve your life and improve yourself. Be that change. Life will be better and healthier then. Take care of you first, if you are happy everybody will goanna come and sit with you, because you will have that happiness in you and you will have that calmness in you. Do that and change your life guys and have fun with your life. So mobile these days are just chaining us to the big black hole to our own life. Change it and take care.

Forgiveness

Yes, we should forgive. We should always forgive. There are many times when we don't forgive people for their mistakes and we keep on taunting them for their mistakes, it's not good. If we don't forgive how will we attain good days with that same person? Forgiveness is something which brings us vast of happiness. It will make your burden on head so light and easy. Which you always keep within you. The inside you. So, forgive, we should always know that God is merciful, if we ask for forgiveness? He gives. So why become so hard on it. Forgiving people is grace in great.

Kneeling down will not make you down if you have done some mistake or hurt someone. Always be down to earth. Then happiness all around begs you to be with you. If happiness you need forgiveness you have to give. Simple and easy? Why not does something which will make you happy? As well as others. "I love you" say to yourself and think to resolve the grudges. Fill that hole to happiness. Not to dig deep in it while not forgiving. Do not please others, but be down to others and be soft. Your actions will lead them to understand and your love within it.

I hope, this is understood. Try that and release yourself from that burden. Do that and see what happens next. You will feel happy and you will enjoy yourself. You will feel light.

You are an amazing person, remember that! Never ever be upset for small things in life. Think bright and be bright. If someone is not going according to your way because it is just their way! Change your own way. Although we cannot stop them infact if we stop them, the more pressure comes on us. So, release. Ask God; observe that he is with you. The answer will come, but always have patience. You need to just have a happy life by forgiving people or you just forgive yourself and forget the negative stuff within you. So, forgive and enjoy. Big days are coming over.

I hope these words will make sense. And we should forgive more then to spoil ourselves! Right? Enjoy it by forgiving. Make a room for the new. Do concentrate in your life and let it go.

Fearless

Always be fearless. The more you will be fearless the more your frequency of positivity will flow, take risks.

Why fear when everything is according to our own actions committed. I have seen many people build fear in them. But remember always it is always God who will take you out from all your fears. Remember that!

In life, if you ever feel fear, just remember lord who has created you. It is not always your friends who will take care of you. Those who are not blessed with good friends. Some may ignore you at the time of help you need. So, what to do then? Do not fear take the support of lord in whichever religion you are. Be there. Who always helps the helpless?

Second read books, because books are your best friends, it is always said. Books make you to forget your present situation and encourage you. Life is full of happiness, why waste on people who are not helping you, be easy. Grow yourself.

Alone you can do many things. Many good ideas come when we are alone. Instead build yourself. We are not alone. We seem to think that. We have many things to do if we make that belief in ourselves. Make yourself so strong that no one can tear you apart. Have always fear of God. And we don't know where we are going in life. It is always to be considerate and courageous. And that comes when you are alone. You build yourself more and more.

Be fearless. No matter what goes on? Be fearless! Have courage in you. Search more and more good things to build instead sitting alone and build fear in you. Go, get that, do not fear, take those steps move forward do not look back. You have more good things waiting in line. Cheer up man, go ahead. Go through all the waves come in. Chase your dreams. Create them. It is within you to create your dreams. Make your life fearless. Not to depend on anyone then to be fearless.

Be Organised

We should always be organized in whatever we are doing and going to do. Plan your day, not from the night which is already going to pass. But from the starting of the morning because that is the new day for you to spend. Be organized because it makes more things better. It makes things more valuable and organized. Those who follow the rules of their lives by being organized are the gems of their life. Being organized makes you perfect in your decision-making.

We have many desires in life. Your desires will come to you to the right time doesn't mean that we should stop dreaming. Dream big instead. The desires will be fulfilled. In addition, be easy, because everything comes at the right time, so why get upset?

Believe, that Believe in you is very powerful.

If you believe anything, you can have in your life. The power of our desires. Some principles and rules if we follow, it is called success. Have faith. Organize your work, your family desires and personal care. Through the principles of your life, you can be more organized. This leads to success. Convince yourself for your better future. Quit your old habits and step into the future of success by organizing yourself. Take out the junk in you. Fortune is always waiting for you if you were organized. So be organized.

Be Active

We should always be active because the more we will be active, we will be able to live life fullest. If we keep on being lazy, we will not be able to be the person, which we always wanted to become. Walk more; join any activity, which will make you energetic like join any gym or something, which will make you fresh and active. Do more convenient activities. Be Active stand up at your work place to take a pause from your chair do some fifteen minutes exercise which will make you happy and active. Get any pet at home. Pets always show owners to be active, as they demand.

Find someone to be active with. Some friends who go to parks for walks or go to any sports activity. It is important. Improve your steps for better life ahead. Anyone can benefit by being active. So why not we be Active? Improve your running. Improve your body. BE fit and BE active. Have good food mostly the food which is cooked at home because that is healthy and most important we don't know if we are eating outside food that is healthy for us or not. So always have home cooked food that is fresh and healthy.

Be active because it is good for your health. Why waste life in laziness. Be active. Do warm ups. You can be active by taking good meals and telling your mind to wake up. Stop grudging yourself for being a pig on the bed all the time, wake up from this dream and move, be active. Enjoy your life by being active. Practice your life to make it better. Encourage others to be active too. Leave your office desk and enjoy fresh air outside. Why waste this time, start from today! Enthusiast your life which has so much to do. We waste our life by being lazy. If we not be looking at our self what we will do for others then. So be active. Take out few extra times from your busy schedule and do some activity.

Leave your TV or phones and go for walks or running. That is beneficial. These things make you feel happy. So, try and enjoy and BE ACTIVE.

Balance!

The balance in life. It is important to have a balanced life. There are times when we need to make all our things balanced. Sometimes it becomes easy and sometimes it gets unbalanced. So here, we always wanted to Balance our work, home, children need, food, money and many more things comes along. How it happens. Start your day with a smile and a positive attitude forgets the bad world in your life for a while and starts your crimson day with a shiny smile. Be as specific as you possibly can. There should always be a goal in life.

Goal setting

In addition, setting of smart goals in life in order to balance your life.

Goal setting is perhaps the first step towards self-development.

Self-development is the process of achieving and expanding our full potential. Self-development should not stop later in life we need to keep moving forward. Taking personal responsibility for your own learning and development of acting. Goal setting ideally involves establishing specific, measurable, attainable, realistic and time-targeted. Always needs to make sure that your goal which you set has a greater chance of being accomplished than a general goal. So always have specific goal inside you so that you can balance your life.

Be SMART. BAD example of a smart goal is ' I want to lose weight'

GOOD example of a smart goal is ' I want to lose 20kg by 15th of July or any date you would like to add when you read this line. I will spend 20minutes on a tread mill, perform half an hour of cardio and half an hour of aerobics per day and I will eat starchy carbohydrates only twice a week.' that will be the smart goal to balance your days for this example and life; similarly it is with your other work and home duties. At every point in goal setting, make sure that you are realistic.

You have to choose that, otherwise you won't be able to achieve it. Make sure you do decide wisely. Low goal exerts low motivational force. Your goal should be bound within a time-frame. Make sure you set a high goal for yourself. Write down your goal in a positive mind frame not in a negative mind frame. Each morning when you wake up read your goals with a positive self-talk and see where you will go. So always have a goal and make your life balanced.

9 789358 191615

Printed by Libri Plureos GmbH in Hamburg, Germany